IT'S TIME TO SHUT THAT DOOR

PASTOR DR. CLAUDINE BENJAMIN

Published by:

Editor: Cleveland O. McLeish (Author C. Orville McLeish)

ISBN: 978-1-965635-60-5 (paperback)

DEDICATION

To every person who has ever opened a door they later regretted.

To the ones who knew better but didn't do better, yet God still kept you.

To the prayer warriors who shut doors in silence.

To the pastors, leaders, intercessors, and hidden gatekeepers who guard the atmosphere, even when no one says thank you.

To those who had to close the door on people they loved, habits they enjoyed, and environments they were once comfortable in, just to obey God.

This book is dedicated to you.

You are the proof that it's never too late to get your spiritual house in order. You are the living evidence that deliverance is real, that discernment is necessary, and that obedience to God is always worth the cost. Every tear you cried behind closed doors—God saw it. Every internal battle you fought before you said "yes" to God— He honors it. Every time you chose holiness over convenience, purity over popularity, and separation over self, He was glorified in it.

And, most of all, this book is dedicated to the remnant—those rising up in this hour with eyes wide open and spirits on fire, who are refusing to leave any access point open to the enemy. You are the ones who will guard the gates, shut the doors, and raise the standard for generations to come.

Finally, I dedicate this book to my Lord and Savior, Jesus Christ, the One who shut the door on death and opened the way to eternal life. You are the Door, the Gate, the Shepherd, and my Defender.

May everything I write, preach, and release point back to Him.

ACKNOWLEDGMENT

First and foremost, I give all glory and honor to God Almighty, the Author and Finisher of my faith. Lord, thank You for trusting me with this assignment and for walking me through the very doors I had to shut before I could write about them. Your presence has been my guide, Your Word my anchor, and Your Spirit my strength.

To Jesus Christ, my Redeemer and the Door to eternal life—thank You for not only saving me but also sanctifying me. Thank You for closing doors I didn't have the courage to shut on my own, and for opening ones that led me deeper into Your purpose for my life.

To the Holy Spirit, my ever-present Helper—thank You for being my compass, counselor, and revealer of truth. You whispered when I wanted to shout. You convicted when I wanted to compromise. You comforted when I felt the sting of separation. This book is birthed by Your wisdom and written under Your breath.

To my family, thank you for your patience, prayers, and unwavering love. To those who supported me when I had to pull away to hear God clearly, your grace made space for this book to be born. I honor you.

To the spiritual leaders, mentors, and intercessors who have poured into me, prayed over me, and challenged me to walk in boldness—your obedience laid the foundation for my own. I thank God for your voices in my life.

To every reader, this book is for you. Thank you for turning the pages with an open heart. Whether you're in the middle of a battle, just came out of one, or are preparing for a greater level of spiritual awareness, I honor your hunger for truth. May every chapter minister to your spirit, empower your walk, and embolden your decisions.

And, finally, to those who once misunderstood my silence, distance, or separation as rejection, it was never personal. I was just learning how to obey God and shut the door.

May this book be a tool in your hands, a sword in your spirit, and a shield at your gates.

ABOUT THE AUTHOR

Pastor Claudine Benjamin is a prophetic voice, teacher of truth, and spiritual warrior called to awaken, equip, and empower the body of Christ. With a mandate to see God's people walk in freedom, authority, and alignment, she ministers with clarity, conviction, and compassion—breaking strongholds and igniting hunger for holiness.

A student of the Word and a yielded vessel to the Holy Spirit, Pastor Claudine carries a special grace to address the hard places—the hidden wounds, silent battles, and unspoken compromises that keep believers bound. Her messages are known for being bold yet healing, confrontational yet redemptive, always rooted in scripture and led by the Spirit.

Pastor Claudine is the author of several impactful titles and is passionate about helping individuals shut the doors to defeat and walk through the ones God has divinely opened. Her ministry is one of restoration, revelation, and revival—for those who are ready to stop cycling and start soaring.

When she's not writing or ministering, Pastor Claudine spends time in prayer, mentorship, and serving the kingdom with integrity. She lives to see God's people whole, filled with purpose, and unshakably grounded in the truth.

> *"I don't write to entertain—I write to equip. If a chain breaks, if a door shuts, if a soul awakens, then the assignment was successful."*
> —Pastor Claudine Benjamin

TABLE OF CONTENTS

INTRODUCTION

We live in a generation where open doors are often celebrated. We chase opportunities, pray for new beginnings, and get excited about access. But what about the doors that need to be shut? What about the doors God never opened, but we stepped through anyway? What about the doors we cracked open with compromise, and now we're fighting battles we were never supposed to face?

This book is a call to spiritual awareness and bold obedience. It's a call to shut the doors that the enemy has used to invade your peace, hijack your purpose, and drain your power. Not every door is from God, and not every open door is an opportunity. Some doors are traps, and some are assignments from hell designed to detour your destiny.

John 10:10 (KJV) - "The thief cometh not, but for to steal, and to kill, and to destroy..."

The enemy only needs an opening—a crack, a moment of vulnerability, a lapse in discernment—to gain entry. But this book is your divine interruption. It's your wake-up call. It's your reminder that as a blood-bought believer, you have the authority not just to close doors, but to shut them and seal them in Jesus' name.

Why This Book?

Because too many people are still bound even after deliverance. Too many are crying out for freedom but refusing to let go of the keys they used to open the wrong doors. This book will help you:

- Identify the doors you've opened knowingly and unknowingly.

- Understand how demonic access points are created and sustained.

- Learn how to partner with the Holy Spirit to close and guard every gate.

- Walk in sustained victory and protect your spiritual territory.

- Break generational patterns and soul ties that have lingered for too long.

It's time to shut the door to distraction. Shut the door to cycles. Shut the door to fear, lust, compromise, rebellion, bitterness, and everything else that has been living rent-free in your soul.

You Were Not Built to Be a Doormat for Darkness

You were born to be a gatekeeper—someone who knows what to allow and what to shut out. You are not helpless. You are not without strategy. You are not without power. Through Christ, you have the spiritual keys to lock out what doesn't belong.

Matthew 16:19 (KJV) - "And I will give unto thee the keys of the kingdom of heaven…"

This is your moment. Whether you've battled with sin, trauma, generational curses, or soul ties, today you draw the line. This is not just a book. It's a manual for spiritual maintenance, a battle cry for discernment, and a blueprint for freedom.

Some doors must be shut forever. And by the time you finish reading this, you will no longer grieve what God has shut—you'll celebrate it. You will no longer be confused by what He has closed—you'll walk confidently in what He has preserved.

The enemy has had access long enough.

The cycle has lasted long enough.

The pain has lingered long enough.

It's time to shut that door and never open it again.

CHAPTER 1

THE DOOR THAT SHOULD HAVE NEVER BEEN OPENED

Some doors in life were never meant to be opened—doors of compromise, sin, trauma, rebellion, disobedience, toxic relationships, and soul ties. Often, what looks like a small crack becomes a wide-open entrance for destruction when we're not vigilant.

The Danger of Curiosity and Compromise

Eve's interaction with the serpent in **Genesis 3** is a clear example of what happens when we entertain the wrong voice. She listened, lingered, and then acted. The door wasn't flung open—it was cracked open through conversation.

> **Genesis 3:6 (KJV) - "And when the woman saw that the tree was good for food, and that it was pleasant to the eyes... she took of the fruit thereof, and did eat..."**

Like Eve, many of us have found ourselves in places we never intended to be—because we opened doors we should have left shut.

One conversation. One compromise. One decision. That's all it took.

Recognizing the Open Doors in Our Lives

Open doors can be:

- Emotional (unforgiveness, anger, bitterness).
- Relational (ungodly connections, toxic influences).
- Spiritual (dabbling in occult, rebellion, disobedience).
- Mental (entertaining lies, fear, depression).

Proverbs 4:23 (KJV) - "Keep thy heart with all diligence; for out of it are the issues of life."

You cannot guard what you're not aware of. Ask yourself: *What doors in my life were opened without God's approval?*

How to Identify a Door That Wasn't Meant for You

1. It pulls you away from God, not closer.

2. It disrupts your peace consistently.

3. It opens the door to bondage, not freedom.

4. It causes spiritual decline or distraction.

1 Corinthians 10:21 (KJV) - "Ye cannot drink the cup of the Lord, and the cup of devils…"

Why It's Time to Shut That Door

Leaving an ungodly door open is like leaving your front door wide open in a war zone. You are exposed to attack. And once the enemy is in, eviction is harder than prevention.

Ephesians 4:27 (KJV) - "Neither give place to the devil."

It's not enough to say you love God. You must close every access point to the enemy, no matter how small, how justified, or how familiar.

Declaration

I declare in Jesus' name that every door in my life that was opened without God's approval is now shut and sealed by the blood of Jesus. I will not entertain the enemy. I will not welcome what God has warned me about. I renounce every agreement, every connection, and every compromise. From this day forward, I will walk in discernment, obedience, and holiness. The door is shut, and it will stay shut!

CHAPTER 2

THE SUBTLE ENTRY OF THE ENEMY

One of the enemy's greatest strategies is to enter our lives subtly. He rarely bursts through the front door. Instead, he looks for cracks—unguarded moments, emotional vulnerabilities, spiritual laziness, or areas where we've become complacent or tolerant of things we once resisted.

2 Corinthians 11:14 (KJV) - "And no marvel; for Satan himself is transformed into an angel of light."

Satan often comes looking like what you prayed for. He disguises danger in desire. He uses people, opportunities, and even thoughts that appear good but leads to bondage. His deception is rarely loud. It's quiet. Clever. Calculated.

The Enemy Waits for an Invitation

The enemy cannot just walk into your life—he needs permission. That permission often comes when we ignore conviction, override God's voice, or engage in things that go against God's Word.

James 1:14-15 (KJV) - "But every man is tempted, when he is drawn away of his own lust, and enticed. Then when lust

hath conceived, it bringeth forth sin: and sin, when it is finished, bringeth forth death."

It's the little things that become big doors:

- One "harmless" conversation that turns into gossip or flirting.

- One late-night text that leads to emotional entanglement.

- One show, site, or song that slowly dulls your spiritual sensitivity.

- One act of disobedience justified by pain, loneliness, or pride.

Song of Solomon 2:15 (KJV) - "Take us the foxes, the little foxes, that spoil the vines…"

We often think we're strong enough to manage the "small" things, but little foxes spoil fruitful lives.

The Enemy Enters Through Unforgiveness and Offense

Unforgiveness is one of the biggest open doors to demonic entry. When we refuse to forgive, we invite bitterness, anger, and torment into our lives.

Ephesians 4:31-32 (KJV) - "Let all bitterness, and wrath, and anger… be put away from you… And be ye kind one to another, tenderhearted, forgiving one another, even as God for Christ's sake hath forgiven you."

Matthew 18:34-35 (KJV) - "And his lord was wroth, and delivered him to the tormentors... So likewise shall my heavenly Father do also unto you, if ye from your hearts forgive not every one his brother their trespasses."

Many people are battling spiritually, not because of witches or generational curses, but because of unforgiveness. That one grudge opened the door.

The Enemy Exploits Spiritual Passivity

When you stop praying, you become vulnerable. When you stop fasting, reading your Bible, and guarding your gates, you leave the door cracked. The enemy waits patiently.

Matthew 26:41 (KJV) - "Watch and pray, that ye enter not into temptation: the spirit indeed is willing, but the flesh is weak."

Spiritual neglect creates an atmosphere where demonic influence can thrive. The more passive you become, the more power the enemy assumes over areas you should be ruling.

1 Peter 5:8 (KJV) - "Be sober, be vigilant; because your adversary the devil, as a roaring lion, walketh about, seeking whom he may devour."

Close the Subtle Doors with Discernment and Discipline

Ask the Holy Spirit to reveal where the enemy has been entering:

- Old wounds not healed properly.

- Entertainment or media that desensitizes you.

- Friendships and alliances that pull you away from your purpose.

- Thoughts and emotions you haven't surrendered.

Proverbs 25:28 (KJV) - "He that hath no rule over his own spirit is like a city that is broken down, and without walls."

You must become a watchman over your own soul. Put up spiritual walls. Guard your gates. The enemy only thrives where he is tolerated.

Isaiah 59:19b (KJV) - "When the enemy shall come in like a flood, the Spirit of the Lord shall lift up a standard against him."

Declaration

I declare that every subtle entrance of the enemy is now sealed by the fire of the Holy Ghost. I close every crack, every access point, and every tolerated lie. I will not be deceived by what looks good but isn't God. I renounce every hidden agreement, every soul tie, and every emotional entanglement. My gates are guarded. My discernment is sharpened. My spirit is watchful. I declare the enemy has no entry and no authority over my life, in Jesus' name!

CHAPTER 3

CLOSING THE DOOR TO PAST WOUNDS

One of the most persistent open doors the enemy exploits is the door of past wounds. These are the pains, betrayals, traumas, and emotional injuries we've carried—sometimes for years—without properly healing. When left untreated, wounds fester into bitterness, insecurity, fear, rejection, and spiritual paralysis.

You can't walk into newness while dragging old pain.

> **Isaiah 43:18-19a (KJV) - "Remember ye not the former things, neither consider the things of old. Behold, I will do a new thing…"**

Before God can do the new, we must shut the door to the old. Healing is not about pretending it didn't happen—it's about refusing to let it rule.

The Enemy Feeds on Unhealed Pain

The enemy thrives where there's unresolved pain. He uses it to:

- Create toxic patterns of thinking.
- Reinforce a victim mentality.

- Keep you in cycles of fear and shame.
- Make you reject people or places God is sending to bless you.

Hebrews 12:15 (KJV) - "Looking diligently lest any man fail of the grace of God; lest any root of bitterness springing up trouble you, and thereby many be defiled."

Bitterness is a spiritual poison that infects not only you but everyone you touch. It grows silently. It thrives in silence. And it opens doors to depression, self-sabotage, and spiritual blindness.

Jesus Came to Heal the Broken

You cannot heal what you're still hiding. Jesus didn't just die for your sins—He died for your pain.

Luke 4:18 (KJV) - "…He hath sent me to heal the brokenhearted…"

Jesus specializes in heart surgery. He doesn't ignore your trauma. He heals it. But healing requires exposure. You must be honest about the wound so He can apply His healing.

Psalm 147:3 (KJV) - "He healeth the broken in heart, and bindeth up their wounds."

The moment you give Jesus permission to go into that hidden place, healing begins. You don't have to fake being whole—God can handle your brokenness.

Letting Go of What They Did

Some of the most painful wounds come from the hands of others. Betrayal. Abuse. Rejection. Abandonment. The natural instinct is to hold on to what they did—to punish them with your silence or withdraw your trust. But forgiveness isn't about them. It's about your freedom.

> **Colossians 3:13 (KJV) - "…forgiving one another… even as Christ forgave you, so also do ye."**

> **Matthew 6:14 (KJV) - "For if ye forgive men their trespasses, your heavenly Father will also forgive you."**

When you forgive, you slam the door on the enemy's ability to torment you with the past.

You Can't Be Free Until You Stop Rehearsing the Pain

Every time you replay what they said or did, you reopen the wound. Healing means choosing not to relive it. It doesn't mean you forget—it means you stop giving it power.

> **Philippians 3:13b (KJV) - "…forgetting those things which are behind, and reaching forth unto those things which are before…"**

You cannot change the past, but you can refuse to let it steal your future. Today, choose to shut the door on the memories that only bring torment and pain.

Closing the Door Requires Confrontation

You cannot conquer what you refuse to confront. Pray. Journal. Seek counsel. Fast. Take that emotional inventory. Look at the wound and say, *"This stops today."* You may have been a victim, but you are no longer bound. You are free through Christ.

> **2 Corinthians 5:17 (KJV) - "Therefore if any man be in Christ, he is a new creature: old things are passed away; behold, all things are become new."**

Declaration

I declare that every wound from my past is now surrendered to the healing hands of Jesus. I shut the door on rejection, betrayal, shame, and trauma. I will not rehearse the pain or allow it to define me. I choose forgiveness over bitterness, freedom over bondage, healing over hurt. I am whole in Christ. The past no longer has power over me. I am healed, I am free, and I am moving forward in victory— in Jesus' name!

CHAPTER 4

WHEN GOD SAYS "SHUT IT"

There are moments in your walk with God when He gives a clear, divine instruction: *"Shut that door."* It may not always come with a thunderous voice, but it will come with conviction, resistance in your spirit, or the withdrawal of His peace. When God tells you to shut a door, it's not for punishment—it's for preservation.

Revelation 3:7 (KJV) - "These things saith he that is holy, he that is true… he that openeth, and no man shutteth; and shutteth, and no man openeth."

God is the Master of divine access. He opens doors no man can shut and shuts doors no man can open. When He says, *"Shut it,"* it means that door is no longer serving your destiny.

Obedience Shuts the Door to Danger

When Noah built the ark, he obeyed God in something that didn't make sense at the time. And when the flood came, it wasn't Noah who shut the door—it was God.

Genesis 7:16 (KJV) - "…and the Lord shut him in."

Sometimes, God Himself will shut a door you didn't have the courage to close. That relationship. That opportunity. That ministry assignment. That job. And even though it hurts, it's protection.

God shuts doors:

- To preserve what He's birthing in you.
- To protect you from future heartbreak or attack.
- To position you for something greater.

You Can't Pray for New and Stay Attached to Old

God will not pour new oil into old wineskins (**see Luke 5:37-38**). If you keep holding on to what He told you to release, you'll contaminate your future with yesterday's residue.

> **Isaiah 30:21 (KJV) - "And thine ears shall hear a word behind thee, saying, This is the way, walk ye in it…"**

When God says *"shut it,"* He's also saying, *"I'm about to take you somewhere that this door can't follow."*

Delayed Obedience is Still Disobedience

Some doors must be shut immediately. Not after you've gotten closure. Not after you've figured out the next step. Not after you've healed. Now.

> **1 Samuel 15:22 (KJV) - "Behold, to obey is better than sacrifice…"**

When Saul failed to obey God fully, it cost him his kingship. Don't let hesitation rob you of what's next. Trust God's command over your comfort.

Disobedience Keeps the Wrong Doors Open

Every time you disobey God's instruction to shut a door, you invite chaos. Peace leaves. Discernment dims. Confusion increases.

> **Jonah 1:3 (KJV) - "But Jonah rose up to flee unto Tarshish from the presence of the Lord…"**

Jonah thought he could escape the call by going through a different door. But disobedience opened the door to a storm. If you keep the wrong doors open, don't be surprised when storms follow.

When God Shuts It, Don't Reopen It

Once God has made it clear that a door is closed, don't try to pry it back open through prayer, fasting, or emotional attachments. That's not spiritual persistence—it's rebellion.

When Israel tried to go into the Promised Land after God said "No," they were defeated (**see Numbers 14:40-45**).

God's "no" is just as divine as His "yes." When He says, "Shut it," close it—permanently.

Closing the Door Makes Room for His Glory

Closed doors are often divine setups. God won't leave you doorless—He'll open better ones once you're obedient to shut the wrong ones.

> **Psalm 84:11 (KJV) - "...no good thing will he withhold from them that walk uprightly."**

> **Proverbs 3:5-6 (KJV) - "Trust in the Lord with all thine heart... and he shall direct thy paths."**

You can trust the God who shuts doors. He's not trying to limit you—He's preparing to launch you.

Declaration

I declare that every door God has instructed me to shut will be closed without delay, debate, or disobedience. I trust His "no" as much as His "yes." I will not mourn over what God has removed. I will not go back to what He has called me out of. I receive grace to walk away, strength to obey, and peace to let go. I am aligned with heaven's instruction. Every door God shuts is shut forever—and I walk boldly into His divine will for my life, in Jesus' name!

CHAPTER 5

GUARDING THE GATES – MIND, HEART, AND SPIRIT

Every believer has spiritual gates—entry points that must be guarded diligently. These gates include your mind, heart, eyes, ears, and spirit. Whatever enters these gates has the power to influence your thoughts, decisions, and direction. If the gates are unguarded, the enemy has free access to infiltrate your life.

> **Proverbs 4:23 (KJV) - "Keep thy heart with all diligence; for out of it are the issues of life."**

This is not a casual command—it's a strategic charge. Your heart is the control center of your life, and what enters it determines what flows from it.

Your Mind Gate: The Battlefield of Thoughts

The mind is where the enemy launches his fiercest attacks. He plants lies, suggestions, temptations, and doubts to weaken your faith and distort your perception of God and yourself.

2 Corinthians 10:5 (KJV) - "Casting down imaginations, and every high thing that exalteth itself against the knowledge of God..."

Romans 12:2 (KJV) - "Be not conformed to this world: but be ye transformed by the renewing of your mind..."

To guard your mind, you must filter your thoughts through the Word of God. Just because a thought enters doesn't mean it should stay. You must evict lies with truth.

Your Heart Gate: The Wellspring of Life

Your heart is where your emotions, desires, and motivations live. It is deeply affected by what you love, what you allow, and what you tolerate.

Jeremiah 17:9 (KJV) - "The heart is deceitful above all things, and desperately wicked: who can know it?"

An unguarded heart will:

- Chase what feels good instead of what is right.
- Justify compromise.
- Stay attached to what God is trying to remove.

Matthew 5:8 (KJV) - "Blessed are the pure in heart: for they shall see God."

When your heart is pure, you discern God more clearly. But when your heart is cluttered, deception creeps in unnoticed.

Your Eye Gate: What You See Influences What You Seek

What you consistently watch becomes what you desire. The enemy knows that visual temptation is powerful. That's why he floods culture with seductive images, violent scenes, and idolatry.

Matthew 6:22 (KJV) - "The light of the body is the eye: if therefore thine eye be single, thy whole body shall be full of light."

Be careful what you binge, scroll, and stare at. What you watch eventually forms an altar in your life—either unto God or unto your flesh.

Your Ear Gate: What You Hear Shapes Your Faith

Faith comes by hearing (**see Romans 10:17**), but so does fear, doubt, rebellion, and seduction. The voices you listen to influence your direction. This includes music, conversations, podcasts, and even preaching. Not every "Christian" voice is of God.

Mark 4:24 (KJV) - "Take heed what ye hear…"

2 Timothy 4:3-4 (KJV) - "For the time will come when they will not endure sound doctrine… and they shall turn away their ears from the truth…"

You must train your ears to recognize the voice of truth and reject the voice of deception.

Your Spirit Gate: The Core of Your Identity in Christ

Your spirit must remain nourished, aligned, and submitted to God. If your spirit becomes starved through prayerlessness or unrepentance, your discernment will be dull, and your strength will diminish.

Galatians 5:16 (KJV) - "Walk in the Spirit, and ye shall not fulfil the lust of the flesh."

Romans 8:14 (KJV) - "For as many as are led by the Spirit of God, they are the sons of God."

Guarding your spirit means staying in the Word, in prayer, and in fellowship with the Holy Spirit. It also means resisting what drains you and aligning with what builds you.

Strategies for Guarding Your Gates

1. Set daily spiritual boundaries.

Psalm 101:3 (KJV) – "I will set no wicked thing before mine eyes: I hate the work of them that turn aside; it shall not cleave to me."

2. Pray for discernment.

Proverbs 2:3-5 (KJV) – "Yea, if thou criest after knowledge, and liftest up thy voice for understanding; If thou seekest her as silver, and searchest for her as for hid treasures; Then shalt thou understand the fear of the Lord, and find the knowledge of God."

3. Feed your gates intentionally.

Fill your mind and spirit with the Word, worship, truth, and godly counsel.

4. Shut the door quickly.

When something ungodly tries to enter, shut it fast. Don't negotiate with the enemy.

Declaration

I declare that every gate in my life—my mind, my heart, my eyes, my ears, and my spirit—is now guarded by the Word of God and the fire of the Holy Ghost. I reject and renounce anything that seeks to enter my gates and defile my purpose. I will not be deceived, distracted, or defiled. I am a gatekeeper over my soul. I will think on what is pure, listen to what is holy, see what is righteous, and speak what glorifies God. My spirit is strong. My heart is pure. My mind is renewed. The gates are guarded and the door is shut, in Jesus' name!

CHAPTER 6

GENERATIONAL DOORS – CLOSING THE CYCLE

S ome doors in our lives were opened before we were ever born. These are generational doors—spiritual, emotional, and behavioral patterns passed down through bloodlines. While genetics may explain physical inheritance, spiritual patterns often explain the repetitive dysfunction, oppression, or warfare people experience generation after generation.

Exodus 20:5 (KJV) - "…visiting the iniquity of the fathers upon the children unto the third and fourth generation…"

This scripture doesn't mean God is unjust—it means that unrepentant sin leaves spiritual consequences that echo into future generations unless the cycle is broken.

What is a Generational Door?

A generational door is a spiritual access point that allows demonic influence, dysfunction, or destructive patterns to continue in a family line. These doors may manifest as:

- Addictions (alcohol, drugs, gambling, etc.).

- Cycles of poverty or lack.
- Broken marriages or infidelity.
- Anger, violence, or abuse.
- Mental health disorders.
- Witchcraft, idolatry, or occult involvement.
- Religious traditions void of relationship with God.

Lamentations 5:7 (KJV) - "Our fathers have sinned, and are not; and we have borne their iniquities."

You may not have chosen the battle, but you can choose to end it.

Jesus Came to Break Every Cycle

The blood of Jesus doesn't just forgive sin—it breaks curses, chains, and cycles.

Galatians 3:13 (KJV) - "Christ hath redeemed us from the curse of the law, being made a curse for us…"

When Jesus died and rose again, He gave every believer legal authority to renounce, uproot, and shut doors that were opened by former generations.

2 Corinthians 5:17 (KJV) - "Therefore if any man be in Christ, he is a new creature: old things are passed away; behold, all things are become new."

You may have inherited the issue, but you don't have to pass it on. You can be the curse breaker. You can be the first to live free.

Identify the Pattern, Then Break It

What are the recurring issues in your family line?

- Is there a history of early death, divorce, or depression?

- Have several family members battled the same addictions or perversions?

- Is there a legacy of religious bondage without spiritual fruit?

  Hosea 4:6 (KJV) - "My people are destroyed for lack of knowledge…"

Identification leads to revelation, and revelation leads to transformation. Once you see it, confront it with the Word and the authority of Jesus.

Breaking Generational Doors Requires Spiritual Action

1. **Repent on behalf of your bloodline.**

Daniel repented not just for himself, but for his people (**see Daniel 9:4-5**).

2. **Renounce all known and unknown agreements.**

Matthew 18:18 (KJV) – "Whatsoever ye shall bind on earth shall be bound in heaven…"

3. **Apply the blood of Jesus over your lineage.**

Revelation 12:11 (KJV) – "And they overcame him by the blood of the Lamb…"

4. Declare the new pattern.

Start walking in the opposite spirit: purity over perversion, faith over fear, order over chaos.

Build a New Spiritual Legacy

God isn't just concerned with your freedom—He's also after the generations that come from you. Closing generational doors ensures that your children, grandchildren, and spiritual descendants don't have to fight the battles you defeated.

> **Psalm 112:1-2 (KJV) - "Blessed is the man that feareth the Lord… His seed shall be mighty upon earth…"**

> **Proverbs 13:22 (KJV) - "A good man leaveth an inheritance to his children's children…"**

Make the choice to leave a legacy of freedom, faith, and fire, not bondage.

Declaration

I declare that every generational curse, cycle, and pattern ends with me. I repent on behalf of my bloodline and renounce every door opened through rebellion, idolatry, trauma, or disobedience. By the power of the blood of Jesus, I shut every demonic door inherited through my family line. I release healing, holiness, prosperity, and purpose into my generations. My children will not fight what I have defeated. I am the curse breaker, the cycle stopper, and the freedom carrier. The door is shut forever—in Jesus' name!

CHAPTER 7

THE DOOR OF DISTRACTION

D istraction is one of the enemy's most effective and deceptive tools. Unlike open sin, distraction doesn't always look evil. In fact, it often comes dressed in opportunity, busyness, or even ministry. But its true aim is to pull you away from your divine assignment, drain your focus, and delay your destiny.

> **Nehemiah 6:3 (KJV) - "And I sent messengers unto them, saying, I am doing a great work, so that I cannot come down..."**

When Nehemiah was rebuilding the wall, the enemy didn't attack with swords at first—he sent a distraction. The enemy doesn't always have to destroy you if he can just distract you.

What Is a Door of Distraction?

A door of distraction is any person, place, opportunity, emotion, or activity that pulls you:

- Away from your prayer life.
- Away from intimacy with God.
- Away from your purpose and spiritual assignment.

- Away from healthy priorities (family, calling, rest, character).

Distractions don't always look demonic—they often look necessary, urgent, or appealing. That's what makes them dangerous.

> **Luke 10:40-42 (KJV) - "But Martha was cumbered about much serving... And Jesus answered... Mary hath chosen that good part, which shall not be taken away from her."**

Martha was distracted by service and missed presence. Sometimes the door of distraction opens even in ministry. Don't confuse activity with anointing.

Distraction Divides the Mind and Weakens the Spirit

The enemy uses distraction to dilute your spiritual sensitivity. You were once sharp, on fire, discerning—and then distraction crept in. Social media. Drama. Toxic relationships. Overcommitment. Emotional attachments. Comparison.

> **James 1:8 (KJV) - "A double minded man is unstable in all his ways."**

> **Matthew 6:24 (KJV) - "No man can serve two masters..."**

When your focus is split, your strength is drained. When your gaze is divided, your growth is stunted.

Samson: A Mighty Man Distracted by a Wrong Door

Samson was anointed, called, and powerful—but he left the door open to distraction through Delilah. His downfall didn't begin with her betrayal—it began with his distraction.

> **Judges 16:16 (KJV) - "And it came to pass... she pressed him daily... so that his soul was vexed unto death."**

The enemy doesn't always bring destruction all at once. He wears you down with distractions until you no longer have the strength to resist.

How to Recognize a Door of Distraction

1. It interrupts your time with God.

2. It consumes mental and emotional energy.

3. It feels urgent, but bears no lasting fruit.

4. It causes spiritual dryness.

5. It delays what you know you're called to do.

> **Ecclesiastes 3:1 (KJV) - "To every thing there is a season, and a time to every purpose under the heaven:"**

When you're distracted, you live out of season. You become reactive instead of purposeful.

Jesus Was Focused—So Must You Be

Jesus shut the door on distraction often. He withdrew from crowds, avoided unnecessary arguments, and prioritized the Father's will over popularity.

> **Luke 5:16 (KJV) - "And he withdrew himself into the wilderness, and prayed."**

> **John 5:19 (KJV) - "The Son can do nothing of himself, but what he seeth the Father do:"**

If Jesus had to fight for focus, so do you. Not everything that comes to you deserves a response. Not every opportunity is from God. Some are traps wearing titles.

Shut the Door, Refocus the Vision

When you shut the door to distraction, you regain:

- Clarity
- Conviction
- Direction
- Productivity
- Peace

> **Isaiah 26:3 (KJV) - "Thou wilt keep him in perfect peace, whose mind is stayed on thee..."**

God doesn't just want your obedience—He wants your attention. When you return your gaze to Him, everything else falls into place.

Declaration

I declare that every door of distraction in my life is now shut by the authority of Jesus Christ. I renounce every mental, emotional, and spiritual drain. I will not be pulled away from my purpose, delayed by unnecessary drama, or discouraged by comparison. My eyes are fixed. My heart is anchored. My mind is stable. I reclaim my focus. I walk in divine clarity and spiritual sensitivity. The door of distraction is shut—and I am aligned with heaven's assignment, in Jesus' name!

CHAPTER 8

KEYS TO KEEPING IT SHUT

Shutting the door is one thing—keeping it shut is another. Many believers close spiritual doors temporarily but unknowingly reopen them through habit, compromise, or emotional vulnerability. God doesn't just want you to shut the wrong doors—He wants you to lock them with spiritual keys and never look back.

> **Matthew 16:19 (KJV) - "And I will give unto thee the keys of the kingdom of heaven: and whatsoever thou shalt bind on earth shall be bound in heaven:"**

Jesus gave you authority, but authority without application leads to vulnerability. If you don't learn how to keep the door shut, you'll be in a constant cycle of defeat, deliverance, and relapse.

Key #1: Consistent Prayer Life

Prayer is your first line of defense. It reinforces your spiritual boundaries and sharpens your discernment.

> **1 Thessalonians 5:17 (KJV) - "Pray without ceasing."**

Matthew 26:41 (KJV) - "Watch and pray, that ye enter not into temptation:"

When you stop praying, the enemy starts planning. Prayer keeps your spiritual gate fortified and your spirit sensitive to danger.

Key #2: Word Saturation

The Word of God is a spiritual sword and a protective barrier. You can't stand against lies if you don't know the truth.

Psalm 119:11 (KJV) - "Thy word have I hid in mine heart, that I might not sin against thee."

Hebrews 4:12 (KJV) - "For the word of God is quick, and powerful... sharper than any twoedged sword..."

You must not only read the Word—you must live it, speak it, and war with it.

Key #3: Fasting and Discipline

Fasting crucifies the flesh and strengthens your spirit. If your flesh is louder than your spirit, you're vulnerable to reopening doors God closed.

Isaiah 58:6 (KJV) - "Is not this the fast that I have chosen? to loose the bands of wickedness..."

Fasting isn't just for breakthrough—it's also for maintenance. It keeps you aligned, humbled, and spiritually tuned.

Key #4: Accountability and Community

Some doors stay shut because you walk with people who know how to check you, pray for you, and walk in truth.

> **Ecclesiastes 4:9-10 (KJV) - "Two are better than one... For if they fall, the one will lift up his fellow:"**

> **James 5:16 (KJV) - "Confess your faults one to another... that ye may be healed."**

Isolated believers are vulnerable believers. Accountability helps you recognize subtle compromises before they become open doors.

Key #5: Guarding Your Environment

You cannot maintain spiritual purity while walking in a polluted environment. What you allow in your atmosphere eventually enters your heart.

> **2 Corinthians 6:17 (KJV) - "Wherefore come out from among them, and be ye separate..."**

Some doors reopen because you stayed too close to what God said to leave. The enemy doesn't need permission if you're living in compromise.

Key #6: Mental and Emotional Renewal

Some doors remain cracked open due to emotional trauma or mental strongholds. Renew your mind daily. Heal your heart intentionally.

Romans 12:2 (KJV) - "...be ye transformed by the renewing of your mind..."

Philippians 4:8 (KJV) - "...whatsoever things are true... honest... just... think on these things."

You cannot have freedom in your life with bondage in your thoughts.

Key #7: Obedience and Immediate Response

When God says "shut it," don't delay. Delayed obedience reopens doors to danger. God gives grace, but He also expects swift alignment.

Deuteronomy 28:1-2 (KJV) - "If thou shalt hearken diligently unto the voice of the Lord thy God... all these blessings shall come on thee..."

Consistent obedience is the lock that keeps the enemy out.

Stay Alert—The Enemy Returns to Check

Jesus warned that unguarded, swept-clean places can be reoccupied.

Matthew 12:43-45 (KJV) - "...he walketh through dry places... Then saith he, I will return into my house... and taketh with himself seven other spirits..."

Deliverance isn't the end—it's the beginning of defense. You must be proactive about protecting your victory.

Declaration

I declare that every door the Lord has shut in my life will remain shut by the power of the Holy Ghost. I take hold of the keys of the kingdom—prayer, the Word, fasting, discipline, obedience, and discernment. I reject all forms of compromise, deception, and distraction. I will not look back. I will not re-enter what God delivered me from. My gates are fortified, my spirit is strong, and my mind is renewed. The doors are not just shut—they are sealed in the blood of Jesus. Victory is my lifestyle, in Jesus' name!

CHAPTER 9

A HOUSE SWEPT CLEAN, BUT GUARDED

Deliverance is powerful, but it is not the final destination. It is a doorway to discipline. Many believers experience moments of breakthrough, freedom, and cleansing—yet they fall back into bondage because they fail to guard what was cleansed. The truth is this: you can be delivered but still vulnerable if your house is not secured after being swept clean.

> **Matthew 12:43–45 (KJV) - "When the unclean spirit is gone out of a man, he walketh through dry places... Then saith he, I will return into my house from whence I came out... and taketh with himself seven other spirits more wicked than himself..."**

Jesus didn't exaggerate. He revealed a sobering truth: an empty, unguarded life is an open invitation for demonic re-entry.

Cleaning Is Not Enough—Filling Is Required

When the unclean spirit left, the house was empty. It had no occupant. It was not filled with anything new or stronger—no Word, no prayer, no presence of God. Just swept but vacant.

> **Ephesians 5:18 (KJV) - "...be filled with the Spirit..."**

Your life cannot remain empty. If you don't fill your heart with the Spirit, the Word, and worship, the enemy will attempt to reoccupy the space he was evicted from.

Colossians 3:16 (KJV) - "Let the word of Christ dwell in you richly…"

Letting the Word dwell richly means filling your house with truth, light, and authority that blocks all darkness.

Freedom Without Fortification Is Futile

Freedom without guarding it is like cleaning a house and leaving the front door wide open in a dangerous neighborhood. The enemy is not creative—he is consistent. He circles back to test your gates.

1 Peter 5:8 (KJV) - "Be sober, be vigilant; because your adversary the devil, as a roaring lion, walketh about, seeking whom he may devour…"

Guarding your spiritual house means you live with intentional awareness. You don't drift through life—you watch, pray, and stand on guard.

Fill the House with God's Presence Daily

You must make room for the Holy Spirit to dwell. Create an atmosphere that welcomes Him and repels darkness.

Psalm 91:1 (KJV) - "He that dwelleth in the secret place of the most High shall abide under the shadow of the Almighty."

When the secret place becomes your residence, demonic spirits will find no entry point. You don't just need visitation—you need habitation.

Guard Your Clean House with God's Armor

Ephesians 6:11 (KJV) - "Put on the whole armour of God, that ye may be able to stand against the wiles of the devil."

The armor isn't optional—it's essential. Guard your house by:

- Wearing the helmet of salvation (protect your mind).
- Holding the shield of faith (block lies and fiery darts).
- Wielding the sword of the Spirit (declare the Word).
- Girding yourself with truth (stay grounded in righteousness).

Do Not Reopen What God Has Closed

Once a house is cleansed, the enemy will often use your memory, emotions, and circumstances to entice you to reopen a shut door. You must resist the urge to re-engage with what God delivered you from.

2 Peter 2:20 (KJV) - "For if after they have escaped the pollutions of the world... they are again entangled... the latter end is worse with them than the beginning."

The most dangerous thing a delivered person can do is return to what once enslaved them. God's mercy cleanses you. Your obedience keeps you clean.

Keep the Fire on the Altar Burning

The house that is filled with worship, prayer, and devotion becomes a fortress. The altar in your life must never go out.

> **Leviticus 6:13 (KJV) - "The fire shall ever be burning upon the altar; it shall never go out."**

Keep the fire burning by:

- Daily time in the Word.
- Continual prayer and thanksgiving.
- Avoiding compromise.
- Staying connected to the body of Christ.

Declaration

I declare that my life is not just swept clean—it is filled, fortified, and guarded by the power of the Holy Ghost. I renounce every spirit that once occupied my life and shut every door that gave them access. I will not return to bondage. I will not leave my house empty. My atmosphere is filled with God's Word, God's presence, and God's fire. I wear the armor of God daily and stand in victory. My house is protected. My mind is renewed. My spirit is empowered. The door is shut, the enemy is evicted, and I am walking in sustained freedom, in Jesus' name!

CHAPTER 10

WHEN GOD SHUTS THE DOOR, LET IT STAY SHUT

There comes a moment in every believer's journey when God not only calls for a door to be closed, but He shuts it Himself. And when God shuts a door, we must trust His wisdom enough to let it stay shut. Too often, we cry over what God has removed, mourn closed opportunities, and attempt to resurrect what He has buried.

But spiritual maturity is marked by this truth: not every closed door is rejection—it is divine redirection and protection.

> **Revelation 3:7 (KJV) - "These things saith he... that openeth, and no man shutteth; and shutteth, and no man openeth."**

What God shuts, no man can open, and that includes you.

God Shuts Doors to Protect You

Some doors look good but hide danger. Some relationships appear promising but carry a compromise. Some jobs, friendships, and environments are appealing to the eye but destructive to your soul.

> **Proverbs 14:12 (KJV) - "There is a way which seemeth right unto a man, but the end thereof are the ways of death."**

God sees what you don't. He shuts doors not to deprive you, but to preserve you. His "no" is always motivated by love.

Don't Reopen What Grace Closed

If God has removed something, disconnected someone, or ended a season, don't go back looking for closure or comfort. Sometimes the door didn't shut because of failure—it shut because of favor.

> **Genesis 19:26 (KJV) - "But his wife looked back from behind him, and she became a pillar of salt."**

Lot's wife longed for a door that God had permanently closed. Her backward glance became her final mistake. When God shuts the door to a place, person, or pattern, it's time to move forward without regret.

The Ark Door: A Door of Finality

> **Genesis 7:16 (KJV) - "...and the Lord shut him in."**

When Noah entered the ark, God shut the door Himself. No one else could open it. Why? Because judgment was coming, and separation was required. God didn't allow Noah to keep the door open for public opinion, emotional appeal, or sympathy.

When God shuts a door, it's not up for negotiation. It's a holy act of divine sovereignty.

You Can't Walk Through Open Doors While Clinging to Closed Ones

To walk in your next, you must release your last. God cannot pour out new oil into old wineskins.

> **Luke 5:37-38 (KJV) - "And no man putteth new wine into old bottles…"**

Clinging to yesterday will contaminate your tomorrow. Closed doors often prepare you for greater doors, but not if you're still trying to pick the lock of your past.

> **Isaiah 43:18-19 (KJV) - "Remember ye not the former things, neither consider the things of old. Behold, I will do a new thing…"**

God's Closed Doors Are Often Mercy in Disguise

Sometimes God's greatest protection is unanswered prayer. That relationship you wanted? That promotion you chased? That platform you thought you needed? God saw the unseen consequences and intervened in mercy.

> **Romans 8:28 (KJV) - "And we know that all things work together for good to them that love God…"**

Faith is trusting God when the door remains shut. It's declaring, *"God, I trust You, even when I don't understand."*

How to Respond to God's Final "No"

1. Worship through the shut door.

Job 1:20 (KJV) – "Then Job arose, and rent his mantle, and shaved his head, and fell down upon the ground, and worshipped."

2. Pray for alignment, not explanation.

Psalm 143:10 (KJV) – "Teach me to do thy will..."

3. Refocus your attention forward.

Philippians 3:13 (KJV) – "...forgetting those things which are behind..."

4. Trust that better is on the way.

1 Corinthians 2:9 (KJV) – "Eye hath not seen... the things which God hath prepared for them that love him."

Let His "no" build your trust. Let the closed door increase your dependence. Let the shut place reveal His sovereignty.

Declaration

I declare in Jesus' name that I will not grieve over doors God has shut. I release every relationship, opportunity, and season that is no longer aligned with my purpose. I will not look back. I will not return. I will not try to open what heaven has sealed. I trust God's sovereignty. I trust His timing. I trust His hand even when I don't understand His plan. The door is shut, and my future is secure. I walk forward in power, peace, and divine purpose. The old is gone. The new is here. In Jesus' name. Amen!

CHAPTER 11

SHUT THE DOOR OF THE PAST

Let Go So You Can Grow

Philippians 3:13-14 (NKJV) - "Brethren, I do not count myself to have apprehended; but one thing I do, forgetting those things which are behind and reaching forward to those things which are ahead, I press toward the goal for the prize of the upward call of God in Christ Jesus."

We often hear the phrase, *"Let bygones be bygones,"* yet so many of us live each day tethered to yesterday. The truth is, your future cannot fully unfold while your focus remains locked on what happened behind you. Paul, the apostle who penned most of the New Testament, understood this powerful principle. Despite his past as a persecutor of the church, Paul embraced the grace of God and boldly declared, **"One thing I do...forgetting those things which are behind."**

Paul wasn't implying that memories are completely erased, nor was he saying that past lessons have no value. He was declaring a deliberate, spiritual decision to no longer allow past experiences—whether painful or prideful—to hinder his present and future walk with God. In order to **"press toward the goal,"** the past had to be put in its proper place.

Letting Go of Past Hurts

Pain has a way of becoming a permanent guest in our hearts when we don't release it. The betrayal, rejection, abandonment, or abuse you experienced might have left emotional scars, but those scars do not define your identity or your destiny. Holding on to offense only binds you to the very people and circumstances that wounded you.

Jesus taught us in **Matthew 6:14-15** to forgive if we want to be forgiven. Forgiveness isn't about saying what happened was okay—it's about choosing not to let it control you anymore. Shutting the door on the past includes closing the access point where hurt once ruled, and allowing healing to begin. Unforgiveness is a weight that slows you down in your spiritual race. It anchors your soul in a storm long after the winds have ceased.

REFLECTION QUESTION

> What past hurt do you keep replaying in your mind, and how has it affected your forward progress?

Releasing Past Failures and Mistakes

Everyone makes mistakes. But for many, the guilt and shame of past decisions become a prison of self-condemnation. Whether it's a failed relationship, a bad financial decision, or a moral failure, God's grace is greater. **Romans 8:1** reminds us, **"There is therefore now no condemnation to those who are in Christ Jesus..." (KJV).**

God is not holding your past against you when you've truly repented. He desires to use even your failures as part of your testimony. But you must first shut the door of regret. Like Paul, acknowledge where you were, but don't stay there. Move forward with purpose, knowing that God can still bring beauty from your ashes (**see Isaiah 61:3**).

REFLECTION QUESTION

Have you allowed past mistakes to define your identity more than God's promises?

Don't Get Stuck in Former Successes

Sometimes it's not just pain or failure that traps us—it's our past victories. Maybe your ministry was thriving in a previous season, or you had an incredible breakthrough years ago, and you've been trying to relive that moment ever since.

The danger of nostalgia is that it can cause you to idolize a moment and miss what God is doing now. Israel kept looking back to Egypt when God was leading them to the Promised Land. Lot's wife looked back and turned into a pillar of salt because her heart was stuck in a place God had already called her out from (**see Genesis 19:26**). Even success must be surrendered to God so that pride doesn't hinder your next level of growth.

REFLECTION QUESTION

Are you holding onto a past success so tightly that you're missing God's present instruction?

You Can't Enter a New Season Carrying Old Baggage

Imagine trying to walk through a narrow door while carrying three large suitcases. Spiritually, this is what it looks like when we try to step into God's new season while dragging the weight of unforgiveness, regret, guilt, pride, or nostalgia.

Jesus said in **Matthew 9:17** that new wine must be put into new wineskins. You cannot pour fresh purpose into an old mindset. The old has to be discarded to make room for the new. Shutting the door of the past is not just about what you leave behind—it's about preparing to receive something greater.

Declaration

"I will no longer be held hostage by my past. By faith, I close the door to pain, failure, and even former glories. I embrace the new thing God is doing in my life!"

Pressing Forward with Purpose

The word "press" in **Philippians 3:14** indicates intentionality, effort, and persistence. You can't press forward while casually clinging to old disappointments. Pressing requires your full attention, your faith, and your focus. Growth doesn't happen accidentally. It happens when you make a conscious decision to release the old and reach toward what lies ahead.

What lies ahead is not just another day—it's destiny. Purpose. A higher calling. But to walk in that calling, you must learn the art of spiritual closure.

You can't expect to soar into your future if you're still chained to your past. Let it go. Shut the door. And don't look back.

Prayer

Father God, thank You for the gift of today and the promise of tomorrow. Please help me to close the doors in my life that no longer serve my purpose. Heal every hurt, forgive every failure, and release me from anything that would hinder my growth. I surrender the weight of my past to You and choose to press forward toward the calling You've placed on my life. Strengthen me to walk boldly into the future, free from the bondage of yesterday. In Jesus' name. Amen.

CHAPTER 12

SHUT THE DOOR OF FEAR AND DOUBT

Faith Cannot Thrive in Fear's Shadow

2 Timothy 1:7 (KJV) – "For God has not given us a spirit of fear…"

F ear will paralyze you and prevent progress. Shut the door on doubt so you can open the door to bold obedience. Fear and doubt do not come from God, but they often come through open doors we've left unguarded—doors of insecurity, trauma, unbelief, or past disappointments.

Fear is not just an emotion—it's a spirit that wants to keep you from walking in power. It wants to replace confidence with confusion and swap faith for hesitation.

Fear Is a Spirit—And It Must Be Rejected

Fear is not a personality trait. It's not just being "careful" or "cautious." It is a spiritual force designed to steal your voice, stall your progress, and suffocate your faith.

When Paul says, **"God has not given us…"** he's implying we've accepted something He never sent. If God didn't give it, why are you still living with it?

> **Romans 8:15 (KJV) – "For you did not receive the spirit of bondage again to fear, but you received the Spirit of adoption…"**

Fear Paralyzes, Faith Mobilizes

- Fear says, *"What if I fail?"* — Faith says, *"God is with me even if I fall."*

- Fear says, *"You're not enough."* — Faith says, *"His grace is sufficient."*

- Fear builds walls, while faith builds bridges.

- Many people are not disobedient—they're just paralyzed by the fear of what obedience will cost.

> **Joshua 1:9 (KJV) – "Have not I commanded thee? Be strong and of a good courage; be not afraid, neither be thou dismayed: for the Lord thy God is with thee whithersoever thou goest."**

Doubt Is a Silent Thief of Destiny

Doubt doesn't always shout—it whispers quietly in the back of your mind. It often sounds like logic, realism, or humility but it's actually unbelief in disguise. Doubt questions what God said by magnifying what you see.

You cannot walk by faith and stare at the storm at the same time.

James 1:6-7 (NKJV) – "…he who doubts is like a wave of the sea… let not that man suppose he will receive anything from the Lord."

What You Tolerate Will Dominate

- You can't counsel fear—you must confront it.

- You must shut the door to fear the moment it knocks, or it will take up residence in your spirit.

- Fear tolerated becomes bondage accepted.

- When God calls you, He also empowers you, but fear will always try to silence the call.

Psalm 34:4 (NKJV) – "I sought the Lord, and He heard me, and delivered me from all my fears."

Open the Door to Bold Obedience

- Boldness doesn't mean the absence of fear—it means you move in spite of fear.

- David still faced Goliath. Esther still entered the king's court. Peter still stepped out of the boat.

- What's the one thing God has asked you to do that you keep putting off out of fear or uncertainty?

Acts 4:29 (KJV) – "And now, Lord, behold their threatenings: and grant unto thy servants, that with all boldness they may speak thy word."

Prophetic Challenge to the Church

If fear has been driving the decisions in your life, today God is calling you to evict it.

— Shut the door on fear of failure.
— Shut the door on fear of rejection.
— Shut the door on fear of not being enough.
— Shut the door on the need for constant clarity.

God doesn't always explain—He expects you to trust.

Reflection Questions

1. Where has fear held you back from full obedience?

2. What would your next step be if fear was not a factor?

3. Are you more focused on what might go wrong than on what God has promised?

Declaration

Today, I shut the door on fear and doubt. I am not ruled by anxiety, hesitation, or uncertainty. I am filled with power, love, and a sound mind. I will walk boldly in faith, knowing that if God called me, He will also carry me. Fear has no place in my next season!

CHAPTER 13

SHUT THE DOOR OF TOXIC RELATIONSHIPS

Not Everyone Can Go Where God Is Taking You

1 Corinthians 15:33 (NKJV) – "Do not be deceived: "Evil company corrupts good habits.""

Some doors lead to cycles of hurt, compromise, or stagnation. Close relational doors that consistently pull you away from God's purpose.

Every relationship is a door. Some doors lead to healing, purpose, and destiny. Others open into cycles of pain, compromise, and spiritual delay. Who you walk with can determine whether you rise or remain. One of the most spiritually mature things a believer can do is evaluate the relationships in their life, and shut the doors that are toxic to their growth.

Relationships Have Direction—They're Either Pulling You Closer to God or Further Away

- Paul gives a warning: **"Do not be misled."** Why? Because it's easy to justify toxic connections out of history, loyalty, emotions, or fear.

- Some people are not bad, but they are bad for your assignment.

- You can't run with vision while tethered to someone who's stuck in confusion, compromise, or complacency.

  Amos 3:3 (NKJV) – "Can two walk together, unless they are agreed?"

Toxic Relationships Produce Spiritual Contamination

- Toxic relationships produce emotional instability, mental exhaustion, and spiritual dullness.

- They drain your energy, challenge your convictions, and introduce unnecessary drama.

- You start second-guessing what God said because you're listening to voices He never approved.

  Proverbs 13:20 (NKJV) – "He who walks with wise men will be wise, but the companion of fools will be destroyed."

The Danger of Delayed Separation

- Abraham could not fully walk into the promise until he separated from Lot (**see Genesis 13**).

- Samson's calling was compromised by his connection to Delilah (**see Judges 16**).

- Judas stayed close to Jesus physically but was far from Him spiritually, and ultimately, his betrayal caused destruction.

- Delayed obedience to sever toxic ties will always cost more in the long run.

2 Corinthians 6:14 (NKJV) – "Do not be unequally yoked together with unbelievers..."

Not Everyone Is Assigned to Your Destiny

- Jesus ministered to the multitudes, discipled the twelve, and confided in three.

- Stop giving full access to people who were never meant to sit in your inner circle.

- God is calling some of you to create boundaries with people who constantly mock your calling, drain your spirit or distract your focus.

Matthew 7:6 (NKJV) – "Do not give what is holy to dogs; nor cast your pearls before swine..."

Disobedience in Relationships Can Stall Your Progress

- Many people cry out for a breakthrough but remain connected to bondage.

- God said to shut the door, but you left it cracked.

- Every time you try to move forward, that old influence pulls you back in.

- You can't walk in spiritual authority while tolerating toxic loyalty.

Prophetic Challenge to the Church

God is getting ready to elevate you, but your elevation requires relational separation.

— Shut the door on gossip circles.
— Shut the door on friendships built on sin, not sanctification.
— Shut the door on emotionally manipulative connections.
— Shut the door on people who are familiar with your past but hostile toward your future.

Reflection Questions

1. Are there relationships in your life that pull you away from God's plan?

2. Have you ignored the Holy Spirit's prompting to release someone?

3. What boundary do you need to establish to protect your spiritual walk?

CHAPTER 14

SHUT THE DOOR TO SIN AND COMPROMISE

You Cannot Win with the Enemy Still Inside the Camp

S in opens spiritual doors to bondage. True success and freedom require separation and consecration.

Romans 6:12-13 (NKJV) – "Therefore do not let sin reign in your mortal body, that you should obey it in its lusts. And do not present your members as instruments of unrighteousness to sin, but present yourselves to God…"

Sin is not just a "mistake"—it is an invitation to the enemy to invade your life, influence your decisions, and interrupt your destiny. You cannot walk in victory while living in compromise. There comes a moment in every believer's life when they must draw the line, close the gate, and say, "No more access."

Sin Is a Ruler—Not Just a Deed

- Paul says: **"Do not let sin reign…"** meaning sin doesn't just want to visit, it wants to rule.

- Sin desires a throne in your heart, mind, and body.

- If you leave the door open, it will take control.

Genesis 4:7 (NKJV) – "If you do well, will you not be accepted? And if you do not do well, sin lies at the door. And its desire is for you, but you should rule over it."

Compromise Is the Silent Killer of Spiritual Progress

- Compromise doesn't always look like rebellion—it often looks like justifying what God never approved.

- A little lie here, a little pride there, a little disobedience in the name of grace—and suddenly, we're spiritually numb.

- The enemy doesn't need you to fall all at once—he just wants you to slowly drift.

Song of Solomon 2:15 (NKJV) – "Catch us the foxes, the little foxes that spoil the vines, for our vines have tender grapes."

Sin Opens Spiritual Doors to Bondage

- Every act of willful sin gives the enemy legal ground to operate in your life.

- You're praying for a breakthrough, but you're entertaining behaviors that block your own blessings.

- Some delays aren't demonic—they're caused by disobedience.

  Galatians 5:9 (NKJV) – "A little leaven leavens the whole lump."

You Can't Carry Purpose and Play with Poison

- God has called you to be set apart.

- Sin distorts your identity, weakens your witness, and blocks your ability to walk in spiritual power.

- You cannot fight giants with dirty hands and expect divine victory.

- You can't say *"Lord, use me"* while still clinging to what He told you to leave behind.

  2 Timothy 2:21 – "Therefore if anyone cleanses himself... he will be a vessel for honor, sanctified and useful to the Master..."

Consecration Is the Key to Clarity and Power

- God is not asking for perfection, but He requires submission and separation.

- Consecration is the decision to set yourself apart for God's purpose, even when culture celebrates compromise.

- Holiness is not legalism—it is alignment with the heart and character of God.

Hebrews 12:14 (NKJV) – "Pursue peace with all people, and holiness, without which no one will see the Lord:"

Prophetic Challenge to the Church

This is not the hour to play with sin—it's the hour to slay it.

— Shut the door to secret sin.
— Shut the door to casual compromise.
— Shut the door to entertainment that desensitizes your spirit.
— Shut the door to relationships that drag you back into cycles you have already left.

God can't bless what you're not willing to surrender.

Reflection Questions

1. Is there a hidden area of compromise that you've allowed to remain?

2. Are you offering God your whole heart—or just the parts that are convenient?

3. What is the Holy Spirit convicting you to release today?

Declaration

Today, I shut the door on sin, compromise, and double-mindedness. I refuse to give the enemy access to my life. I choose consecration over compromise, obedience over comfort, and purity over popularity. I am a vessel set apart for God's glory, and I walk in power, not pollution!

CHAPTER 15

SHUT THE DOOR ON NEGATIVE SELF-TALK

Your Words Shape Your World

Proverbs 18:21 (NKJV) – "Death and life are in the power of the tongue..."

Stop replaying internal lies that say you're not enough. Align your words and thoughts with what God says about you. The most dangerous voice in your life is not the one around you—it's the one within you.

Negative self-talk is the inner dialogue that repeats lies, insecurities, and labels that God never gave you.

It's time to silence that inner critic, shut the door on self-defeating thoughts, and start speaking life over yourself.

What You Speak Becomes What You Believe

- Words are not just sounds—they are seeds.

- Every word you speak, especially over yourself, is sowing something into your future.

- If you continually say, *"I'm not good enough… I'll never change… God can't use me,"* then you're shaping a life out of fear, not faith.

James 3:6 (NKJV) – "And the tongue is a fire, a world of iniquity. The tongue is so set among our members that it defiles the whole body, and sets on fire the course of nature; and it is set on fire by hell."

The Power of Internal Agreement

- The enemy doesn't have to defeat you if he can get you to speak defeat over yourself.

- When you agree with lies internally, you live like they're true externally.

- You begin to limit your prayers, lower your expectations, and disqualify yourself from what God has already made available.

Numbers 13:33 (NKJV) – "There we saw the giants (the descendants of Anak came from the giants); and we were like grasshoppers in our own sight, and so we were in their sight."

Silence the Voice of the Old You

- Negative self-talk often flows from past pain, rejection, or trauma.

- The old you wants to remind you of who you were. But the new you must rise in confidence in who you are in Christ.

- You are not your past. You are not your mistakes. You are not your failures.

- Shut the door on the internal voice that's echoing yesterday when God is declaring your tomorrow.

   2 Corinthians 5:17 (NKJV) – "Therefore, if anyone is in Christ, he is a new creation; old things have passed away..."

Align Your Words with God's Truth

- If God says you are chosen, loved, healed, and called— why are you still calling yourself broken, forgotten, or unworthy?

- The Word of God must become the standard for your self-talk.

- Speak His Word over your mind until your mind agrees with your mouth.

   Joel 3:10 (NKJV) – "Let the weak say, 'I am strong.'"

Your Confession is Connected to Your Destiny

- The Israelites wandered for 40 years in the wilderness, not because of God's limitation, but because of their own confession of unbelief.

- They were free from Egypt, but still bound in their thinking.

- Likewise, many today are saved, but still stuck because they have not yet shut the door on their negative narrative.

  Hebrews 10:23 (NKJV) – "Let us hold fast the confession of our hope without wavering…"

Prophetic Challenge to the Church

This is not the season to talk yourself out of the blessing.

— Shut the door on *"I'm not good enough."*
— Shut the door on *"God can't use someone like me."*
— Shut the door on *"Nothing ever works out for me."*

God says you are more than a conqueror, so speak like it!

Reflection Questions

1. What negative phrases do you find yourself repeating that contradict God's Word?

2. Are you speaking life over your future or death over your destiny?

3. What truths from scripture do you need to declare daily to reshape your thinking?

Declaration

Today, I shut the door on every lie I've told myself. I silence the voice of fear, failure, and insecurity. I will speak life, victory, healing, and purpose. My words will agree with God's Word, and my life will align with the Word of God.

CHAPTER 16

SHUT THE DOOR TO THE ENEMY'S ACCUSATIONS

You Are Not What You've Done—You Are Who God Says You Are

> **Romans 8:1 (NKJV) – "There is therefore now no condemnation to those who are in Christ Jesus, who do not walk according to the flesh, but according to the Spirit."**

Satan is the accuser. Don't allow condemnation to keep you from walking boldly in your calling.

One of Satan's most effective strategies against believers is not always temptation—it's accusation. The enemy knows if he can't keep you in sin, he'll try to keep you in shame. But there is a difference between the conviction of the Holy Spirit and the condemnation of the devil. Conviction leads to repentance and restoration. Condemnation leads to guilt, retreat, and disqualification.

Satan Is the Accuser—But God Is the Advocate

- The devil is described in scripture as the accuser of the brethren (**see Revelation 12:10**).

- He constantly brings up your past, magnifies your flaws, and whispers, *"You're not worthy."*

- But while Satan accuses, Jesus defends. He pleads your case not based on your perfection, but on His righteousness.

  1 John 2:1 (NKJV) – "And if anyone sins, we have an Advocate with the Father, Jesus Christ the righteous."

Condemnation Chains You to What God Has Already Forgiven

Condemnation keeps replaying the same scene from your past, causing you to feel stuck in cycles of regret. It tells you, *"You'll never change,"* even when God says, *"You're already new."*

You cannot walk boldly in your future while dragging the weight of a forgiven past. Shut the door on spiritual guilt trips.

Isaiah 43:25 (NKJV) – "I, even I, am He who blots out your transgressions for My own sake; and I will not remember your sins."

Your Identity is not Defined by Failure but by Redemption

- God does not call you by your mistake—He calls you by your name.

- Paul persecuted the church, yet became one of its greatest apostles.

- Peter denied Jesus, yet preached the sermon that birthed the church.

- God specializes in redeeming rejected vessels.

  2 Corinthians 5:21 (NKJV) – "For He made Him who knew no sin to be sin for us, that we might become the righteousness of God in Him."

Walk in Boldness, Not in Shame

- Shame causes you to hide. Boldness calls you to rise and serve.

- When the enemy reminds you of your past, remind him of his future—and of your position in Christ.

- You were not just set free from sin; you were raised to reign with Christ.

  Hebrews 4:16 (NKJV) – "Let us therefore come boldly to the throne of grace..."

Don't Let Yesterday's Accusation Rob You of Today's Assignment

- God's grace didn't just forgive your sin—it equipped you for purpose.

- The enemy's goal is not just to remind you of who you were—it's to rob you of the impact you're meant to have now.

- You must shut the door on the lies that say:

    ∂ *"You're too broken."*
    ∂ *"You've messed up too many times."*
    ∂ *"You're disqualified."*

Romans 11:29 (NKJV) – "For the gifts and the calling of God are irrevocable."

Prophetic Challenge to the Church

Shut the door to the courtroom of shame.

— You've been justified by grace.
— Your identity is not on trial.
— You are not defined by your darkest moment.
— You are defined by the finished work of the cross.

Reflection Questions

1. What accusations from the enemy are still echoing in your heart and mind?

2. Do you believe you've truly been forgiven or are you still carrying the guilt?

3. What would it look like to walk boldly and freely in your calling today?

Declaration

Today, I shut the door on every accusation of the enemy. I silence the voice of guilt, shame, and condemnation. I am who God says I am—redeemed, chosen, and called. I will walk boldly in my purpose, confident in the grace that covered me and the blood that has cleansed me!

CONCLUSION

THE DOOR IS SHUT – NOW WALK IN VICTORY

You've come through ten powerful chapters where God has revealed the importance of spiritual doors—what must be shut, what must be guarded, and how to remain free. But this book isn't just a call to close doors—it's a call to live differently once they're shut.

Too many believers walk in cycles instead of victory because they never truly let go of what God told them to shut out. But you are not called to cycle—you are called to soar. You are not called to visit freedom—you are called to live in it.

> **Galatians 5:1 (KJV) - "Stand fast therefore in the liberty wherewith Christ hath made us free, and be not entangled again with the yoke of bondage."**

As you move forward, remember this: *shutting the door is a lifestyle, not a one-time event.* It means daily choosing to guard your gates, close access to sin, shut down distractions, and refuse to reopen wounds, habits, or soul ties.

Let your shut doors be the testimony that you are no longer who you used to be. Let every sealed place preach the sermon: *"I've been delivered, and I'm not going back."*

You are now the doorkeeper of your destiny.

Guard it well. Walk in wisdom. Be sensitive to the Holy Spirit. Trust God's "no" as much as His "yes." And never forget—you're not doing this alone.

The One who helps you shut the door is the same One who will walk with you into your next open one.

> **Revelation 3:8 (KJV) - "…behold, I have set before thee an open door, and no man can shut it…"**

Step into the New by Shutting the Old

> **Isaiah 43:18-19 (NIV) – "Forget the former things; do not dwell on the past. See, I am doing a new thing! Now it springs up; do you not perceive it?"**

Every New Season Begins with a Door Decision

You cannot enter into the next if you're still tangled in the last.

God is calling you higher, deeper, and forward—but before you step into the new thing, you must make some intentional choices about what doors stay open and what doors must close.

The same door that gives you access can also give the enemy a foothold if left open carelessly.

- New beginnings require bold endings.

- You can't keep petting what God told you to crucify.

- You can't walk through God's open door while still peeking back at the one He shut.

Revelation 3:8 (NKJV) – "I have set before you an open door, and no one can shut it…"

God Is Doing a New Thing—But You Must Let Go of the Old

- Many cry for change but refuse to release what's hindering them.

- God doesn't pour new wine into old wineskins (**see Matthew 9:17**).

- If you keep entertaining the past, you'll miss what's springing up right in front of you.

- He says, **"Do you not perceive it?"**—because you can miss the new if you're still mourning the old.

2 Corinthians 5:17 (NKJV) – "If anyone is in Christ, he is a new creation; old things have passed away…"

This Is a Call to Decision, Not Just Inspiration

Today isn't just about feeling motivated—it's about making a life-altering choice.

It's time to:

- Shut the door of the past.
- Shut the door of fear and doubt.
- Shut the door on toxic relationships.
- Shut the door to sin and compromise.
- Shut the door on distraction, negative self-talk, and the enemy's accusations.

This is your moment of divine alignment, but doors don't close themselves. You must choose to shut them in faith and walk away in freedom.

Prophetic Declaration Over the Church

Today, I choose to shut every door that does not lead to God's purpose for my life. I shut the door to my past, to fear, to shame, to sin, and to everything that keeps me from fulfilling God's call. I step forward into my new season with boldness, focus, and faith. No more delay. No more distraction. No more defeat. The door is shut and the way is open!

Sealing Every Door

Heavenly Father, in the name of Jesus, I thank You for the strength to shut every door that You never intended for me to walk through. I repent for every open access point—knowingly or unknowingly— that has given the enemy entry. Today, I declare divine closure.

I close the door to sin, fear, compromise, distraction, and generational cycles. I close the door to toxic relationships, wounded places, and past trauma. I apply the blood of Jesus to every gate of my life—my mind, my heart, my body, my home, and my spirit.

Holy Spirit, fill every area that has been swept clean. Dwell in me. Teach me to guard what has been given. Remind me daily of who I am and where You are taking me. I refuse to look back. I embrace the future You've prepared. I declare: *the door is shut and sealed by heaven.* In Jesus' name. Amen.

SCRIPTURE REFERENCE INDEX

Spiritual Discernment and Guarding Gates

- Proverbs 4:23
- 1 Peter 5:8
- Matthew 26:41
- Colossians 3:16

Breaking Cycles and Generational Curses

- Exodus 20:5
- Galatians 3:13
- Daniel 9:4-5
- Lamentations 5:7

Distraction, Focus and Purpose

- Nehemiah 6:3
- Luke 10:40-42
- Matthew 6:22-23
- Isaiah 26:3

Freedom, Deliverance and Sustained Victory

- Matthew 12:43–45
- Galatians 5:1
- 2 Peter 2:20-21

- Leviticus 6:13

Obedience and Trusting God's Timing

- Revelation 3:7-8
- Genesis 7:16
- Isaiah 43:18-19
- Romans 8:28

www.ingramcontent.com/pod-product-compliance
Lightning Source LLC
LaVergne TN
LVHW021537080426
835509LV00019B/2700